TODAY
IS THE FIRST DAY OF MY
FUTURE

A Story of Hope

Dionna Reeb, M.Ed

ISBN 978-1-63630-922-4 (Paperback)
ISBN 978-1-63630-923-1 (Digital)

Covenant Books, Inc.
11661 Hwy 707
Murrells Inlet, SC 29576
www.covenantbooks.com

CONTENTS

ACKNOWLEDGMENTS

I want to thank those who have played a part in my recovery. First off, Mike, my husband, who created the "hospital at home" program for me and loves me more than life itself. He has changed my life in so many ways, and I love him dearly.

The second most important player in my world is Ray S. He was there for me night and day, and sometimes in the middle of the night too.

Jeff and his parents, Ken and Kerry D, who visited me in the hospital and took me to church on Sundays week after week.

My mom, Nancy H, who tried so hard to be a good mom and often advocated for me in the middle of mental health breakdowns.

My sister, five years younger than me, Libby, who saw way more than a teenager should have ever had to see and dealt with way more than any young adult should ever have to deal with.

My mother-in-law, Nancy R, who is always there for me and will sit back and quietly listen.

And finally, Sylvia H. She is my dear Christian friend who keeps me tethered to the Word of God and reminds me often that God is sovereign.

INTRODUCTION

I am sitting down to reflect my past, present, and future. Starting around age ten, my life was chaotic. One crisis followed by another. But as I look back, I see that God was with me, is with me, and will always be with me. He has demonstrated his grace over and over. If He can make something good come out of the stupid and dangerous decisions I've made, He can do the same for any hurting soul.

My goal with this book is to open the window of my past and to let God blow my hurts, my pain, and my disappointments out the window. And as He does that, I hope others can grab hold of the hope I now have. Today is the first day of my future!

PROLOGUE

Mental Illness—An Analogy

I am walking along the beach feeling calm and serene. Then I come upon a cave; I am curious. I walk inside. At first it is light and colorful. Then as I go deeper into the cave, I begin walking through a marsh with my feet sticking into the mud. It gets harder to go forward. As I continue to walk, there are so many paths to take, all toward darkness. I go though one entrance and continue my journey through the mud. It gets darker and darker; the mud is getting thicker; the walls are slimy. As I go along, I begin to get scared. It is dark, and I realize I am lost. I begin desperately seeking the light from which I came. I begin frantically running in the darkness, running into the cave walls. My feet keep getting stuck. I fall several times. It gets more and more difficult to continue on.

All of a sudden, I realize that I am no longer sinking in the mud; I must have fallen through a hole of some sort. In the process, I break my leg. I lie there gasping, ready to give up all hope of getting out of the cave. Realizing that there is life outside the cave, I manage to pick myself up. As I step on the broken leg, I scream in agonizing pain. Someone, I don't know who or how, heard me. I hear my name—someone is looking for me.

Finally I am found. I feel a surge of hope! I will be okay. The rescue worker loads me in a gurney, and I am taken to the hospital. The doctor asks me, "What hurts?"

I respond, "My leg. Can you fix it?"

"Well," I am told, "after x-raying it, I can see it is broken."

I ask, "Will you fix it?"

The doctor responded, "We are going to send you home with some aspirin. Just hang in there for a few weeks, and maybe then we'll repair the damage."

I am now crying. "But it hurts. Can I at least have something for the pain?"

"Here is some aspirin. Come back in a few weeks."

I come back in few weeks. My leg is now turning colors. I can barely tolerate the pain. It is agonizing. A dull throbbing at all times and sharp pain when I try to walk." Again I ask, "Can you fix it?"

And the doctor answers, "Not today. We do not think it is necessary to do anything right now."

Fortunately, I lived through the pain of cutting away the dark parts of myself. I learned to stop cutting, stop drugging, and stop acting out. I have learned to manage my emotions and to contact my psychiatric providers when I first notice a major change in my sleep pattern as that is the first indication I am going up or down. I have learned to advocate for myself without being demanding.

All of this is mainly because of my relationship with God and my husband. God has kept me safe in the throes of illness and Mike has helped me with making better decisions. What I really want to say is this:

Life is good! Today is the first day of my future!

THE BEGINNING
OF MY ILLNESS

Shadow of Things to Come

Am I possessed, or am I crazy? I asked myself this question often. I was about ten years old when the first crazy thought entered my head. I was sitting in the chapel at my school, on the floor, pressed up against the white stone wall. We were practicing for our spring play. I generally felt sad, but the darkness that overcame my young mind was too much for me to handle. I was overcome with the desire to smash my head on the wall and see my bloody brains all over the nice stone wall. I began crying as I pressed my head against the wall as hard as I could.

After the practice, I went to talk to my teacher. In tears, I told the teacher that I was possessed by demons. She dismissed me with a simple solution, "Put your favorite Bible verse on your bedroom wall. You will feel better." I came back to her the next day, telling her of my violent nightmares. I had dreamed that demons were in my house, and I was afraid that they would destroy my Bible. Understand, my Bible, even at ten years old, was my most treasured possession. It was my only connection to God. My teacher simply said, "Read your Bible and pray before you go to bed; you will feel better."

And I did not feel better. Although I attended church three times a week, read my Bible, and prayed, I did not feel better! Throughout my childhood and up into my mid-adulthood, I asked for help—often. I was prayed for, prayed over—and one couple even prayed to speak to the demons inside of me. It made no difference. I have accepted Jesus as my Savior more than twenty times and have been baptized four times. I had hands laid on me many, many times. It made no difference. I read my Bible, studied my Bible, and even took three years of Bible college. It made no difference.

And then one day it occurred to me that the problem may not be spiritual. So if I am not possessed, I have to ask, "Am I crazy?"

Throughout my childhood, I released my emotions by banging my head on the wall. No one knew about this, not even my family. I banged my head so hard and so often that I, to this day, have scalp sensitivity.

When I was about twenty years old, I left college housing to live with a family from church. On a particularly bad afternoon, I was sitting on my bed with the contents of my school supply box spread out on the bed. My heart was beating hard, and my stomach was tied in knots. I wanted to smash my head so badly. But I knew I could not as V, the mother, was home that day. I felt like I would just burst into a million pieces if I did not bang my head *right now*!

Then it happened! I saw a box cutter sitting among the pencils and pens. *I wonder.* I needed a release, but I knew I could not bang my head. I picked up the box cutter and ran it along my skin, lightly. *Could I?* I pondered the notion of cutting myself as that would not be loud and no one would even know.

Just about that time, J returned home from high school. She came into the room, and she asked if I was okay. When I told her no, she wanted to go tell her mother so she could help. We began to argue, and then I just seemed to snap. I grabbed the box cutter and threw the blade into my right forearm. Blood spurted in a stream, so I grabbed my sock to cover it. When that was not enough, I grabbed my bath towel. J left the room, and I sat down to catch my breath and then call my mom to take me to the ER.

My mom arrived about an hour later. I had sworn J to silence, and I quickly ran out to meet my mom at the car. Now in today's world, everyone has heard of people cutting. Today, cutting is as anorexia was in the '80s: it's almost a fad among young folks. Back in the early '90s, however, it was virtually unheard of. My mom asked how I hurt myself. I admitted that I had cut myself on purpose. I could tell my mom was horrified. I simply kept apologizing, and my mom said nothing more until we got to the hospital.

In silence, we drove to the hospital. When we arrived, my mom told the triage nurse what happened, and the nurse took me right back to a room. As the doctor began numbing the cut area, he asked if I was trying to kill myself. I told him, "No, but that sounds like a good idea." I said it sarcastically, but it was the truth. I had only told one person in my whole life that truth.

When I was sixteen years old, a junior in high school, my tormented soul could take no more, and I told my mom simply, "I need help. I want to die." Tears fell from my eyes. My mom responded by screaming at me, telling me how selfish I was. I remember one statement that crushed me to the core, "You must really hate me if you want to die." It was never about her. And I never said those words again until...

That day—a day I mourn over. It was the day I started my life as a mental health patient (I was twenty years old). It was a future of uncertainty, darkness, and utter craziness. It was the first day of my future.

The Hospital

As the doctor stitched up my arm, he asked me questions to determine my level of safety. "How long have you been hurting yourself?" "Do you think about death?" "Do you have a plan to kill yourself?" "What is your plan?" I was not very cooperative and answered as briefly as I could. I told him that I normally banged my head, but today, I decided to try cutting. Yes, I thought about how I would kill myself. I did not have a plan, but the desire was very strong.

The doctor finished with my physical wounds and began to address the emotional pain. He said that he thought it would be best if I was admitted to the psychiatric unit for safety and an evaluation. I was not about to say yes to that! In the end, I guess he wore me down, and I said I would go.

As I was led to the psychiatric unit, I heard screaming. Several staff were pushing a gurney with a restrained lady on it. The lady was screaming, "Just let me die!" What little did I realize, later that night, I would be that screaming lady.

I had been assigned to a one-to-one staff for my safety. Basically, it meant that I had a "babysitter" that was within arm's length at all times. I was on the highest level of suicide watch. Well, having a male baby sitter when I wanted to shower flat out made me angry! I began screaming at him to leave me alone.

I continued to escalate until eight behavioral health technicians (BHTs) and a nurse came to restrain me with both physical and chemical restraints. Physical restraints consisted of leather cuffs on each wrist and each ankle, and those cuffs are tied to the bed. Chemical restraint was a shot in the butt of Haldol, Benadryl and Ativan. Within minutes, I was so drugged that I could no longer fight, and I slept, still restrained to the bed.

When I came to, I realized I was no longer restrained but still had the "babysitter" right outside the door to the isolation room where I was. I was told that I would be confined to the isolation room with the one-to-one sitter just outside the door. I could only leave the isolation room to use the restroom. I was not allowed to have anything except my bedding. I was not even allowed my glasses. And I am blind without my glasses! But I had nothing to look at anyway.

After a few days in the isolation room, I was allowed to go back to my regular room, still with the babysitter. I began attending groups, and I had individual counseling every day. I was so new to the psychiatric world. But I knew I wanted help. I was severely depressed, to the point of having suicidal thoughts almost continuously.

Groups were designed to help teach us coping skills, and individual therapy was designed to untie all of the symptoms and hopefully come up with solutions that would help. I did not find any of it much help. I was started on Zoloft (anti-depressant) and Depakote (mood stabilizer), plus I could have Ativan (anti-anxiety) every four hours as needed. It would take a trial of eight weeks before we knew if the cocktail would help.

Hospitalizations are rather brief, so after two weeks, I was released with my medications and told to follow up with my psychiatrist within seventy-two hours. And so I did. After meeting with Dr. P, I was assigned to a therapist in the office. I met with the doctor every four weeks and with the therapist every week.

My meds were changed every time I saw the doctor! Zoloft, Prozac, Wellbutrin, Depakote, Tegretol, Prolixin, Haldol, Effexor, Ativan, Klonopin, Ambien, Lamictal, Vistaril, Thorazine, Lithium, Geodon, Topamax, Lexapro, Zyprexa, Xanax, Luvox, Effexor, Risperdal, Clozaril, Seroquel—oh so many medications.

Some made me so drowsy that I would fall asleep in my car on a hot summer's day in Arizona. Some made me feel so wired that I thought I could just pop out of my skin. My fight to find medications that worked would last for fifteen years. But in the meantime I was oh, ever so depressed.

Therapy was probably the worst thing I ever did. I opened up my heart and soul and all of the yuckies came pouring out of me. Problem is, once I let all that stuff out, I spend the rest of my years sorting through it all. I am grateful for the therapists I had as they were patient with me and ultimately taught me coping skills that I needed to lead the life I now lead.

Well, that first hospitalization was only an introduction of me to the psychiatric world. I quickly became a revolving door in the private mental health sector. I followed a pattern. I would be in the hospital, and my meds would be changed. Within a week or two, I was tired of lock-up and started stating that I felt fine so they would release me. Within a very short period of time, I started cutting again. That would lead me back to the ER for stitches and back to the psychiatric ward. For several years, I was a revolving door in the ER and psychiatric hospitals.

My History of Cutting

Sitting on the cement bench outside of the grocery store, I carefully touched the razor blade in my right hand. I imagined what it would be like to push the blade down and actually cut my skin. I continued to fondle the blade and lightly ran it across my left leg. And then I did it. I nicked the skin and bled just a bit. Then I did it again and again. I had several small cuts on my thigh, then I really did it. I ran the blade crossways on my thigh hard enough to make a deep incision that would later be stitched.

Half-elated and half-mortified, I decided I better stop and walk home. The blood soaked my shorts, and later that evening, my mom took me to get the bad cut stitched. They wanted to stitch some of the nicks I had made, but I was stubborn and just kept saying, "I only need this one stitched." It was six stitches—the second of many, many times I would be in the ER or urgent care getting stitched up.

My mom did not understand my need to cut. In fact, there are very few that understood my need to cut. Sometimes I would cut superficially, and other times I would cut very deep. When I cut superficially, I often played with the drops of blood that would appear on my skin. I even drew pictures in a drawing journal with my blood.

Often my depression would be so dark that I needed to see the blood to know I was still alive. Other times the depression would be so painful that I needed the cutting to control the emotional pain with physical pain. And still, other times, I would cut so that I would have an excuse to go to the hospital. At least someone talked to me. I was so desperately lonely. Regardless of the reason, cutting was my go-to behavior when I wasn't doing well.

One Friday night, I was feeling particularly depressed and lonely. I was in my car, parked in the parking lot of the local ER. I wasn't sure if I should go in. I played with the blade in my hand. And then, before I could lose courage, I took a deep swipe at my leg, near the ankle. I had some gauze with me and wrapped it up. It was a deep gash—deeper than I had ever done. I walked into the ER, and the RN recognized me and took me back after I signed in. She unwrapped the wound and said, "Wow! That's deep!" The doctor came in and looked at it. He told me it would take two layers of stitches. One layer to sew up the tissue and one layer to sew up the skin.

The doctor asked the standard questions to assess my level of safety. It was not good. He decided that I needed to be inpatient in the psychiatric ward again. I went, but I was not happy about it. All of the ins and outs of the psychiatric hospitals was wearing on me, and I was getting tired! I just wanted to be out of pain. I just wanted the suffering to stop.

COURT-ORDERED
TREATMENT

"**H**elp me!" I knocked on the priest's door by my house. "I have razor blades in my purse, and I want to kill myself." I was a wreck. I was seriously suicidal and scared. The priest opened the door and said, "Just a minute," and he closed the door. He must have called 911. He opened the door and said, "Let's talk here in the light," as he led me to the street light. Just as I got to the street, six or so, cop cars came swerving around the corner with their lights on. I tried to run, but I was so scared I was stuck in my place.

All I can remember is that one of the police officers talked to me and another talked to the priest. The police officer asked me how old I was. I told him I was twenty-two. He asked me where I lived. I told him I lived around the corner with my mom. He assessed my level of safety and determined that he wanted to take me to County Hospital. I said, "Absolutely not!" But as he talked to me, he convinced me to go and just talk to someone. The line had been crossed. I got to the hospital, and there was a lady behind a thick glass barrier, and she said, "Voluntary or Involuntary?"

I said, "Neither, I just want to talk to someone." Meanwhile, the police placed me on a seventy-two-hour court-ordered evaluation. I ended up on unit four of the psychiatric floor.

The day room was quiet. No one was in the big, bright room. All that was in this room was rows of tables and chairs. Everything took place in this room. Groups, Arts and Crafts, meals, medications, TV time, and socialization.

I was led through this room to my sleeping quarters as it was past midnight. It was a room with five other patients. That was the big difference between private hospitals and court-ordered facilities: private hospitals only have two to a room. Court-ordered facilities put four to six in a room. And believe it or not, the court-ordered facility rooms are smaller! I didn't care though. I just went and laid down on the empty bed and went to sleep.

The next day, I woke up to the announcement that it was med time. I had not seen a doctor yet, so I figured I would not have any meds yet. But I was wrong. I took the little cup and downed it. Who cares anyway? I was a little fearful as I had heard stories about County Hospital. Amazingly, I fit right in. That's a scary thought. When you fit into the psychiatric ward, you know you are messed up!

I made friends with one of my roommates. K and I came up with a brilliant idea. We closed the door to our room and pushed all six beds from the door to the back wall, making it impossible for the staff to open the door. We were having a grand time; staff kept knocking on the door and asking us to open the door. We went and hid in the closet. I finally gave into the staff's request. They had chainsaws and were coming in one way or another. I did not want to be responsible for the damages. K, however, was very upset with me. She wanted to play it out until the end.

Somewhere along the way, I met my lawyer. I did not understand the court-ordered treatment process, but my lawyer said it would be best to consent to ninety days inpatient per year total court-ordered treatment. What I did not understand is that basically this is a plea deal. If I had either fought the order or said I would go voluntarily to a private facility (as I did have private insurance), I may not have ended up in the Arizona State Hospital. But my lawyer did not even give me a chance. He just told me to consent to the order. The order I agreed to was ninety days inpatient per year total, but what I did not know is that once court ordered, they can easily amend the order to keep you longer. After two weeks in County, I was transferred to the Arizona State Hospital (ASH). I was in ASH for a total of seven months.

This was the place for the worst of the worst. And here I was. How did I end up here? Today was the first day of my future.

Sitting in the dayroom the first day, I looked around. It was a large area which was a dingy white and full of blue rubber/plastic chairs. These chairs were heavy duty so they could not be thrown, is my guess. The TV was a nineteen-inch TV that sat in a plexiglass cube so that, again, it could not be thrown. No one really watched much TV because there was no way to change the channel, which was regularly on the Public Broadcasting Station (PBS). There was a shelving unit full of books and puzzles. The room was rather empty and cold, but they were after safety, not day room of the year.

"Code yellow, unit 2. Code yellow, unit 2." What I didn't realize is that there was a scuffle going on. M refused her medications that morning. She was sitting in the chair opposite the room from me. Rather quickly, there were several staff members from other units standing around M. M tried to bolt, but the staff was quick. They grabbed her arms and legs and took her down to the ground. Then they carried her to the isolation room and four-point restrained her (two on the hands, two on the feet) with leather cuffs that are tied to the bed.

That scene was a common occurrence. Takedowns happened anytime someone was acting like they were unsafe or were uncooperative. It would be something that I would endure often. "Code green, unit 2. Code green, unit 2." I was raging through the room, throwing anything I could find to throw. I was screaming that I hated the hospital and wanted to go home. I turned a table on its side. By then I was surrounded by staff. Before I knew what was happening, the staff members were taking me down.

They grabbed my arms and legs and took me to the ground in no time flat. Then they carried me to the isolation room and gave me the "takedown cocktail" (Ativan, Benadryl, Haldol), a big shot in my butt. They continued, undressing me so that all I had on were my underwear and bra. Then they strapped my hands and feet to the bed. Once it was all said and done, I was nearly naked, strapped to a cold plastic covered mattress, and locked in the isolation room with a staff member sitting outside the door.

After four hours, I was released from restraints. Restraints and takedowns often happened to me. I spent time in restraints at least three times per week. Because of that, I could never earn privileges. White. Blue. Green. Gold. As a new arrival, I started off as a white band. The band was my name and hospital information which came in one of the above-four colors.

White—no privileges and restricted to the unit. Blue—can go off the unit with staff supervision. Green—can go off the unit with a gold band. Gold—full privileges and can go off the unit by one's self. Evaluations with the psychiatrist happened once a week, and the band color could only go up at this time. But the band level can go back to white (no matter what color you are) if you are involved in a takedown.

"Code yellow, unit 2. Code yellow, unit 2." Staff began crowding into my room. I was hiding under the bed as far back as I could get. I was sick of getting up at 6:00 a.m. only to sit in the dayroom. They locked the dorms during the day, drugged me to the point I couldn't help but fall asleep; but we were not allowed to sleep in the day room.

As a way of protest, I hid under the bed. I was given a chance to come out peaceably, but I didn't. So the staff that were summoned by the code got down on the ground and pulled me out, kicking and screaming. I was then taken to the isolation room and put in restraints. Purpose accomplished! I got a shot, and I was allowed to sleep while restrained.

The people in ASH were all very different. Some were DTS (danger to self) and others were DTO (danger to others). At one point, I was on a two-to-one (two patients to one staff) with L. L had killed someone in her family and declared incompetent. I was stuck as her roommate and, for all intents and purposes, buddy for the time being. I was afraid of her.

There was, however, one lady I was even more afraid of—D! She was a big lady with the understanding of a small child. I told staff that she had been picking on me. The staff told me to just stand up to her, and she will back down. So that night, in the showers, I walked up to her, naked and wet, and yelled at her to leave me alone or else! I didn't have an "or else" but it sounded good. The next day in the lunch room, I was hit across the back of my head with a lunch tray—it was D. Spaghetti went everywhere. I screamed at her, and I was stripped and put in restraints. D was simply told to go to her room as she was calm.

I was allowed visitors only on the weekends. My mom was faithful to come see me every weekend. She would bring me food from any restaurant that I chose and often came bearing gifts of clothing, shoes, or other essentials. When she came, she would often see me just sitting in the corner of the day room staring straight ahead. I often sat in the corner because that is where I felt safe. I could see everyone and no one was behind me. It was actually more of an emotional safety that I was after rather than physical. I could hold my own physically, but mentally, I was messed up!

On one visit, my mom asked me, "What happened to your chin?" which was Steri-Stripped. I had been involved in a particularly nasty takedown, and the staff had thrown me to the ground, splitting my chin open. There was blood all over me and my sweater. But no worries, we are in a hospital, they can fix it, right?

Wrong! They continued the takedown until I was five-point restrained. This meant both hands, both feet, and my head was tied to the bed. The doctor came in to suture the split chin. He said that they did not have Novocain on the psychiatric ward, so he started stitching me up without it. Yes, I screamed as he put the first stitch in! He told me to calm down, it was only a few little stitches. I required a total of four sutures. Then he left, and I spent the night tied to the bed.

The next day, yet another take down. As they undressed me, they pulled my sweater over my head and ripped out the stitches in my chin. Again, blood all over the place. But they were kind enough to wash the sweater as I spent the next four to six hours in restraints. They Steri-Stripped the gash on my chin.

When I told my mom what had happened, she was furious. She turned around and wrote letters to the president of the hospital, the newspaper, and the Department of Health Services. As with all the other complaints my mom filed, nothing came of it. They said they investigated and found no evidence that I had been thrown to the ground, sutured without Novocain, and/or restrained without good reason. The investigation consisted of reading my chart, which of course, the staff isn't going to write in their guilt. They never interviewed me or other patients that may have seen what happened.

My mom wrote many letters to Department of Health Services trying to get me out of ASH. The hospital staff spoke with my mom at some point, telling her that I was so mentally ill that it was not likely that I would ever leave the hospital. This devastated my mom. She could see the abuses but could not do anything to get me out. Somewhere along the way, my mom told me that the hospital had no intention of releasing me, at least for a very long time.

As I lay in restraints one day, I thought about my life. Being tied to a plastic mattress, nearly naked and severely drugged, was not my idea of a good life. It is definitely not what I had ever imagined for my future. I cried out to God. In my dark little world, I felt a sense of hope. I thought to myself, "I'll be damned if I stay here the rest of my life." And *boom*, the formation of my first goal (not ever having been taught goal setting). I decided I would not ever be put in restraints again, and I would work my band levels up so I could eventually go home.

And so I did. I stopped acting out so that I would not be taken down any longer. This was despite of my severe depression that, even with the medications, never went away. I learned the phrase "fake it 'til you make it." While not the ideal patient, I did cool my jets and spent a lot of time writing in my journal and reading my scriptures. It was the only thing that would keep me calm and out of trouble.

I first got to go off the unit with staff. So every morning, I went on the walk around the hospital with staff and other blue bands. It was nice to be out of the unit. I was looking forward to being a green band. This meant I could go on a home visit for the day. And boy, a gold band meant I could spend the weekend at home. I continued focusing on my goal when I felt like acting out. An amazing thing happened—not only was I spending time off the unit, but full weekends at home. One day I was talking to the president of the hospital (for some reason he took a liking to me). He asked if I would like to have my car at the hospital so I could go off site for up to eight hours and do my own thing. I just had to come back in the evening. YES!

After I was able to start going off-site, I decided I would look for a part-time job. Amazingly I landed a part-time job as an assistant manager of a clothing store in the local mall. Wow! Who would have thought? After seven months in ASH, I was deemed not a danger to myself, and they discharged me to my own apartment. Let me make perfectly clear, I may have been deemed not a danger to myself, but I was in no way healed, fixed, or all better! I just started my life as another rotating door in the private hospitals. But at least I was no longer the "worst of the worst." This was the first day of my future.

Getting Help in the "System"

When I was released from the Arizona State Hospital, I was still under court-ordered treatment. I had to go to the county run clinic for a weekly shot of Prolixin and monthly scripts for all my oral med-ications. I entered the system as they changed hands to ComCare.

The weekly visit was beyond annoying. I also spoke with my case manager, J, nearly every day. The scenario went something like this: "J, I just want to die. I can't take it anymore!"

J would say, "Do you want to go to the hospital?" I'd say no, and she would say, "If you are a danger to yourself, I have to call crisis so they can pick you up for the hospital." So I promised that I would not hurt myself if I did not want to go to the hospital. If I did want to go to the hospital, I would have her drive me to a private hospital (not ASH).

God bless J! She put up with me on a daily basis. She never got mad at me. She just had my best interest at heart. She constantly encouraged me to be better. She encouraged me to put the blades away and be productive. She talked me into going back to school.

The culture of the SMI (seriously mentally ill) clinic needs to be touched on. SMI is a legal status which opens doors for various treatments. Back in the days of ComCare, all services were free to SMI clients. Medications (name brand and generic), group therapy, individual therapy, and even social groups. Since then, the services have really been cut back, but we still get the bare essentials (generic medications, peer support, and peer-run groups).

When I went into a clinic, I could count on other patients to acknowledge that I came in. I could count on someone asking me for a cigarette. I could count on someone asking me for fifty cents for a soda. If I had anything to give, I would give it in a heartbeat. And if I did not have it, someone else in the lobby would step up and give the person what they were asking for.

One thing I noticed is, SMI folks are giving. It could be their last fifty cents or their last cigarette, but they would give it to someone who asked. Most of these folks are on SSI (social security supplemental income) or SSD (social security disability). The average income was about $500 a month back in the '90s/2000s, but if a member had something that someone "needed," it would be given. This always amazed me!

The county system has changed hands many times and has been restructured three times since I've been a member (that's what they call us). I don't even really know how the current system works. I just know I get to see the psychiatrist every three months and get my generic medications at no cost.

MY ILLNESS PEAKS

Teen Challenge

Shortly after my release from ASH, I began struggling with cutting again. My mom searched for a program for me that would help. She was put in contact with a program called "Teen Challenge" which was a faith-based drug and alcohol treatment program. My mom talked to the leaders of the program in Georgia and begged them to help me. And they agreed to. They said that the cutting could fall into the category of "addiction," and they accepted me.

In February of 1995, I was admitted to the program. I flew out to Georgia and the leader, T, picked me up at the airport. I was quiet on the way to the house as I did not really want to be there. When I got to the house, it was late in the evening. T took me up to the bedroom which had four bunk beds in it. I was to take the top bunk on the far left-hand side. It's amazing how programs can cram people into a small area.

I unpacked and went to sleep. The next morning, I was shown to my desk. Every day we were to study for six hours. We studied 9:00 a.m. to noon and 1:00 p.m. to 4:00 p.m. The studies were packets on addiction and devotional studies of the Bible. In the evenings, we often gave concerts (which I had to be a part of) to raise funds for the program.

The fast-paced life of studies and singing and going to churches (again, to raise money) was more than I could stand. I found a push-pin in the closet and started scraping my skin with the pin. I could not do much damage, but I drew enough blood to catch the attention of the leader, T. She brought me into the office and told me I was not to be trying to cut myself anymore. I was given a "demerit." For every demerit, you would get thirty minutes of a punishment; such as cleaning the garbage cans with a toothbrush. If they thought I was going to clean the bottom of those large cans with a toothbrush, then they were crazy!

On a Wednesday night, we were invited to go to a Foursquare Church to share our testimonies. I did not feel I had a testimony to share, but T thought differently. When I flat out told her, "No, I don't have a testimony to share," she believed me, but my stubbornness was met with a punishment of sorts. When we got home, T told me to go up to the empty room on the third floor and to pray to God until I spoke in tongues and got my testimony. Didn't she realize that Baptists don't believe in speaking in tongues? I sat up in the room for a while and came back down and told T that I could not speak in tongues. T was not happy!

The next day I was found to be in opposition to the program, so I was kicked out. My mom was called by the staff and was told to order me the next flight home. They told me to pack and to meet them in the van in thirty minutes. So this is where refusal to clean garbage cans and not having any sort of testimony to share gets you...

T drove me to the airport and simply dropped me off (it was about 3:00 p.m.). I knew what airline I was flying, but I had to find out when the flight was that my mom purchased for me. It was not until 8:00 a.m. the next day! And the airport closed at 11:00 p.m. I did not have any money to go to a hotel. I had no choice but to wait out the time outside the airport. Thank heavens for the security guard. He saw me sitting outside and asked if he could help me. I told him my predicament. Being a kind, older gentleman, he allowed me to stay in a small alcove inside the airport. I was told not to move outside that area, or the alarm would go off. I settled in for a nap and woke up at 6:00 a.m. when people started coming in again. And I left Georgia and never looked back. This was the first day of my future.

Electro-Convulsive Therapy

One day—a particularly bad day—when I was about twenty-five, I ended up in Charter Hospital. This was about five years into my mental health career. I ended up with a doctor who thought I was medication resistant. By this point, I had tried just about every medication and several different combinations. Being medication resistant left only one other treatment: ECT (electro-convulsive therapy). I was game. I desperately wanted to feel better. I could not argue with Dr. B that medications did not seem to be helping. So I prepared to stay two to three weeks and have four to five treatments.

I knew nothing of ECT. I did not know anyone who had them; therefore I did not know anyone to ask if they helped or not. The doctor was optimistic. At this point my diagnosis was major depression recurrent. If the ECT stimulated the right neurons in my brain, it would relieve the inner darkness I felt. The night before my first treatment, I was very anxious and could not sleep. I was given Visteril and Ativan to help calm my nerves and help me sleep.

The next morning, I was awakened at five a.m. to get ready for my first ECT. I showered but was not allowed any food or drink because I would be sedated for the treatment. They had told me that I would be given IV medications to relax my muscles and to put me to sleep so that the treatment was not violent, as in the old days. I laid on the bed, and the nurse started an IV. I was rolled into the treatment room and almost immediately sedated. Next thing I knew, I was waking up with the worst headache I had ever had. I was given strong IV pain meds for the headache.

Once I was awake and oriented, I was walked back to the unit. I still had a headache, and I felt quite sick to my stomach. I went back to the unit and promptly threw up all over the day room. The on-duty tech was not happy. She sent me back to my room and told me she would have the RN come talk to me. The nurse gave me medicine for my headache and nausea, and I went to sleep.

I don't remember much else of that time frame. I know I had a total of thirteen treatments in three different hospitalizations. By that point, I lost most of my memory (common side effect) of that time frame. I forgot where I lived, where I worked, and even what I did for a job. So I lost my job, as AT&T did not want to retrain me. And I lost my apartment because it was in a residential program that required I stay out of the hospital. Once again, I was lost.

One positive thing came out of all the craziness of the ECT treatments: I ended up with a very good doctor who closely watched me—before and after the treatments. He said he could see the deep depression I was in before treatment. After a couple treatments, I got better and would be released. But after the last ECT (number thirteen), he did not quickly release me even though I felt better. This is when he said he saw the mixed mania in me. Mixed mania is when there is depression and mania at the same time. This includes symptoms of agitation, irritability, excess energy, short attention span, and lack of sleep. That is when I was first diagnosed as bipolar. I have maintained that diagnosis until this day.

Bipolar Disorder

I want to touch on my life with bipolar disorder. First, the obvious, was the depressive episodes. It was the depressive episodes that normally caused me to be hospitalized because I would get suicidal. In a depressive episode, everything was black. Nothing was good. I slept a lot, ate very little, and cried easily. The depressions were painful to my soul. Sometimes I would just curl up in a ball and cry myself to sleep. Those depressive times were desperate times. I would cut myself, overmedicate myself, or do both.

In one particularly bad depressive episode, I overmedicated on Ativan. I took ten one-milligram tablets. My plan was to take the whole bottle, but I fell asleep. The next day, I woke up and did not realize I was still super drugged. I got ready for work and got in my car. On the freeway, I kept falling asleep because I was so sedated. I hit the median several times. Upon pulling off, one of the cars that had been forming a barrier around me, stopped me at the red light. He motioned me to roll down my window.

He said, "Give me your keys! You are not fit to drive!"

I thought I was being car-jacked. But within minutes, the police were there, asking me questions about my hitting the median so many times. I told them about the Ativan the night before and that I wanted to die. I was fortunate. The police parked my car in a neighboring parking lot, and I was sent to the hospital. I was shocked that I did not get a ticket for DWI, but I guess they figured I was suffering enough.

The manic episodes were so much more fun. I felt on top of the world. I was open and friendly. I had energy and would clean my apartment and organize all cabinets. I would go without sleep and then tackle huge projects around the house (like pruning all the bushes)!

If I was in school, I took advantage of the manic episodes to finish any and all homework for the semester. If I wasn't going to sleep, I might as well study! My biggest problem was in spending money. I would go to Walmart at two a.m. and buy all kinds of stuff for my apartment, clothing for myself, and gifts for my friends. I got so far in debt that I had to go into a debt-consolidation program. It took me five years to pay off all that debt!

On one manic episode, shortly after my marriage to Mike, I had started many cleaning projects but did not finish any of them. I was so proud of myself, as I had cleaned (partially) the kitchen, bathroom, bedroom, living room, and laundry room. I even found where I put the pancake syrup—under the kitchen sink! When Mike got home, all he saw were cleaners and rags all over the house. So proud, I said to him, "I've been cleaning the whole house!"

"I see," he said. Mike was kind. He just left everything, figuring when the mania wore off, I would see what I had done. And I did! Then I really did clean the whole house. But not in one day!

The mixed episodes are when I experienced both mania and depression at the same time. The symptoms of mixed mania for me are: lack of sleep (one night for every three), agitation, irritability, anger, a deep sense of pain and darkness, and frustration.

Mixed episodes are actually the worst of the three. I couldn't sleep, but I was too tired to do anything productive. So I laid in bed and felt sorry for myself. I had just enough energy to be destructive to myself. I felt bad about myself and looked to men to make me feel better. Promiscuity is a big part of mania and mixed episodes. For me, it was mostly in the mixed episodes.

Suicidal Tendencies

In my twenties, my mental health was probably at its worst. At baseline, I was suicidal. Every day I thought about how I could end this miserable existence. Sometimes the suicidal thoughts were like background noise. Other times they were like someone was shouting on a loud speaker.

On Christmas Eve in 1996, I was sitting in church for the service. The communion came around, and all I could hear was, "You can't take that, you are evil! God will punish you!" I got up and walked out of the service. I didn't know where I was going

It was about seven p.m. and I was aimlessly walking the streets of Mesa, Arizona. Tears flowing down my cheeks, all I could hear was "You are evil. You are the worst person ever. You are evil!" Eventually I got picked up by one of our other church members. They asked if they could take me home.

I said, "No! I can't go home!" So they brought me back to their place, where I promptly locked myself in the bathroom.

Eventually the pastor arrived and tried to talk to me. I couldn't talk to him. All I could do was cry. He got me to agree to go home (I lived with my mom at the time). The pastor drove me to the house and came in to talk to my mom. He told her to just let me be and that I would be going to sleep. And I quickly went straight to my room and shut the door.

Trazodone, Benadryl, Ativan, Depakote, Tegretol, Zoloft—my stock pile of drugs. I started downing them, a handful at a time. Once I got 180 pills into me, I felt a sense of peace, and I lay on my bed, ready to face my Maker. That's the last thing I remember, but I will tell you of what happened the next morning.

My mom walked by my bed to check on me, and my head was hanging off the bed. At first she did not think much of it, but then she circled back to place my head back on the bed so I did not get a sore neck. That is when she saw black stuff on the carpet under where my head had been hanging. That's when she started to panic. She tried to wake me up, to no avail. She called out to my sister to call 911.

I was life-flighted from our cul-de-sac to poison control in Phoenix. My mom drove to the hospital. After they had worked on me pumping my stomach, they told my mom that I would be okay once I woke up. Everything I took (they had the empty vials) was dangerous, but since I had survived to that point, I would be okay.

I woke up sometime early the following morning. I could not remember what had happened to me. My entire body ached, and I had a large tube in my throat. I thought maybe I had been in a bad car accident. My hands were tied to the bed so I could not pull out the respirator. A nurse happened to see I was awake and asked me if I knew where I was. I shook my head no.

She said, "You took an excessive amount of medications a couple days ago. You have been in a coma. We pumped your stomach, but you aspirated and much of it went into your lungs. You now have a bad case of pneumonia, which is why you have the respirator breathing for you."

Then I remembered what had happened. I was angry! Angry at myself for not taking enough pills to kill myself. Angry at my doctors for saving me. And angry at God for not allowing me to die.

I stayed in the medical ward for two weeks, healing from the pneumonia. The doctor I had checked on me every single day. He also prayed with me every day. I think that being at a loss for how to help my emotional pain, he did what most Christians do: pray about it. I don't mean to make it seem trite, but because I was depressed to the core, suicidal, and unable to think clearly, prayer just seemed like the last thing in my life that I really wanted to do. Plus, I was still angry at God. But my doctor really tried to help me have peace with God. I never had the heart to tell him that God and I were at opposite ends of a boxing ring, and I was getting pretty beat up. As time went by, I began to look forward to our daily prayers. I still held hope that one day I would be okay.

When I was released, I went back to my mom's house. Still suicidal, I vowed to do it right next time. And six months later, next time came.

One spring afternoon, I picked up my monthly supply of medication. I had ninety Ativan, ninety Tegretol, ninety Depakote, thirty Zoloft, and a few odds and ends. I parked in front of a hotel and walked to a nearby hotel. I figured that if they found my car, they still would not find me. Dressed completely in black to symbolize my utter darkness, I checked into the hotel for three days as that was all the money I had. I figured twelve hours did not do it the first time, so three days ought to do it this time.

I opened the door to my room and poured out my monthly stash. 320 pills in all. Plus I had a large bottle of some kind of fruity alcohol. I sat on the bed and wrote out all the medications I had along with a note about my inner darkness and inability to manage my ever-lasting depression any longer. I started taking handfuls of medications and downing the alcohol. I was going to do it right this time! Finally, I got everything down, and I felt very sick, so I laid down on the bed, prepared to meet God and tell him exactly what I thought of the life he had given me.

I fell into a deep coma. Apparently, during the three days I was in the hotel, I had two heart attacks and passed out on the bathroom floor. The maid found me when she came to clean the room. Amazingly, I was still alive. Meanwhile, during the three days that I was missing, the police had helicopters in the desert looking for me. In the weeks before my actual attempt, I talked about my plan to go to the desert and take all my pills. Once they found me, they let my mom know I was still alive and in Desert Samaritan Hospital.

I did a lot of damage with the medications I took. The doctor said that I should have died within fifteen minutes of taking all those drugs and alcohol. But there I was! Alive. But I was in a deep coma. As days went by, my mom would come to the hospital and just pray I would come out of it. The doctor prepared my mother for the possibility that I would not come out of it. After two weeks in the hospital, they prepared to transfer me to long-term care. The doctor had little hope that I would come out of the coma, and if I did come out of it, I would likely have brain damage.

At about the two-week mark, I just woke up. Being that I was still very much confused, I don't remember waking up. But I do remember the pain in my leg. Apparently, I had fallen asleep with my leg stuck behind me and caused nerve damage. It was very painful! I was on crutches for a month or so. After waking up, they transferred me to the psychiatric hospital. This was the first day of my future.

Everyday Life

Daily life for me was one of deep emotional chaos. I worked part-time jobs in-between hospitalizations. I excelled in retail sales. On the sales floor, I could be anyone I wanted to be. I was outgoing, knowledgeable, and helpful. It was the one place that I could almost feel normal. The longest job I had was at Kinney Shoe Store. I worked from being a cashier, to salesperson, to assistant manager. I worked there for a couple of years.

The biggest problem with working at Kinney's was the never-ending supply of box cutters—my knife of choice! I would be on the sales floor and feel okay, but when I went back to the stock room, I would see two or three box cutters and my anxiety would tighten my throat and pound in my chest. I wanted to feel those blades on my skin. How can one go from feeling good on the sales floor to absolutely crazy in the stock room?

I finally told my boss the truth about how I felt when I saw the blades in the back room. He was a good boss. He did his best to be sure all blades were properly put away in the manager's desk as to not tempt me. That worked well for the most part. Unfortunately, one must choose for themselves not to cut. Knives or blades are readily available.

I often went to Walgreen's Drug Store when in a bad place and buy everything I needed to cut. I bought a box of straight edge razors, gauze pads, rolled gauze, and tape. One had to wonder what the lady checking me out thought to herself. Would she know what I was about to do? Or would she be oblivious? To this day I don't know the answer to that question.

It got to the point that I had a "cutting kit." In my plastic container were blades, bandages, band-aids, and antibiotic ointment. I got so good at Steri-Stripping my deeper cuts that I rarely had to go to the ER for stitches anymore. I pulled out my box a few times a week and wondered how crazy I really was. Normal people don't create a box for cutting and first aid all together. Normal people don't draw pictures in their journal with the blood they drew with the blade. Normal people did not cut in the first place!

I was definitely not normal. I prayed, pleaded, and cried to God to make me normal. I was in a deep dark pit with no way out. It was like someone was reaching down to help me out and I was reaching up to grab on, but we were still a foot apart. There was no hope. There was no light. There was no good.

And yet I kept on going. There were times I would lay on the lawn of the church I was attending and just cry my heart out to God. I imagined that he was literally storing all my tears in a jar as I heard that from the pulpit. I felt so sad, and I did not think God could really store all my tears as there were way too many.

I would often go talk to the pastor or counselor. Counselors would tell me I need to be more active in church. Pastors would tell me I need to accept Jesus as my savior. My Christian friends would tell me to read my Bible more. Such trite advice from people who really had absolutely no clue as to how bad I felt.

I did much of my therapy with Dr. D. He was my college professor in psychology 101. He was always good at listening and helping me work through my issues. Problem was, I had so many issues that it was like a dog chasing its tail. But I have to say, of all the therapists I had over the years, Dr. D was the best one.

I would journal during the week, and he would read what I wrote when we met. He seemed to care about my suffering and truly wanted it to go away. Plus he met with me for a discounted rate because he knew I could not afford his regular rate on a weekly basis. He was so good to me! He even came to my college graduation (different school at that point).

Another faithful friend/counselor was Pastor P. I was introduced to him when I was in ASH. He came weekly to visit, teach, pray, and mostly listen. My mom had started going to his church and told him about me. My mom was used to pastors saying they would talk to me, but Pastor P was the only pastor that actually stuck by me and faithfully met with me weekly for years.

He never said that I just needed to accept Jesus as my savior. He did, however, tell me I needed to live a more Christ-like life. He never tried to fix everything and was really more of a friend and mentor than a pastor.

Brother S was honestly the most faithful, awesome friend anyone could ask for. He is an example of a Christ-like servant if ever I saw one. I called him at 2:00 a.m. in total distress many times, and he would always listen to me and help me to calm down. He was known to drive me to the psychiatric hospital late at night because I could not wait 'til morning. He often kept my toolbox of medications (yes, I had that many) and would administer one week or less at a time, depending on my level of safety.

He often told me he was going to kick me with his hobnail boots if I didn't straighten out. He was teasing of course. I was always trying to quit smoking, so I often brought him partial packs of cigarettes, and he would say, "Should I write this date in pencil?" By the way, I did finally quit about six years ago.

Yes, Brother S was my anchor. God was so good to put him in my life. When everything went off the rails, Brother S was there to pick up the pieces. And as he would just get done solving one crisis, the next one would hit. He once asked me, "What would help you get through the next few hours?"

I said, "Church's chicken." And wouldn't you know it, he brought me Church's chicken and a coke. That really did help! Sometimes it was the little things that would get me through a moment or crisis.

So many times I sat in Brother S's office, in his recliner, and poured my heart out. He listened to my pain. He listened to my sinful mess ups. He listened to my anger about my deep depression. He was just always there for me. I could not have asked for a better person to be put in my life.

His favorite saying when I asked, "How are you doing?" was "I'm a goin' and a blowin'!" And it was so true. He was always busy. But as busy as he was, he always made me feel like I was the only person in his world. He is truly the example of a godly man.

STARTING TO PULL IT ALL TOGETHER

Addictions

When I was in my thirties, I really decided that I wanted to get my life in order. I was tired of the cutting. I was tired of living in pain. I was just worn out. I hit rock bottom. My boyfriend at the time was part of AA and felt that a similar program would be helpful to me. I was put in contact with a lady that would be my first sponsor and who would walk me through the painful process of letting go of addictions.

M, my sponsor, suggested that I go to Narcotics Anonymous (NA) and identify as an addict. She felt that my cutting was an addictive behavior and that I would get the most out of the NA program. M told me that I had to do ninety meetings in ninety days. I committed myself to this as I was serious about getting healthy. I even had a major surgery during my first ninety days, but I attended over a hundred meetings in my first three months.

"Hi, I'm Dionna. I am an addict." I identified as an addict on my first meeting. I listened to the readings and the various speakers. As I listened to the speaker talk about how her life had become out of control because of drugs—that she would do anything to get drugs and to use drugs—I began to identify with her. She talked about hiding her drugs and binging.

And it *hit* me! I was a drug addict. I had never considered this, but the speakers really hit home, describing my life with all the ups, downs, and in-betweens. I was a prescription-drug addict and had never considered this a problem, as I got the drugs from the doctor. I doctor shopped, went to ERs and urgent cares, and would pull my all-time favorite, "This isn't working. Can I have something else?" I managed to build quite the stockpile. When my anxiety got too bad, all I wanted to do was sleep it away. So I took twenty to thirty pills of various sorts to make me not feel the anxiety and then I slept. I did not do this every night, but I did it four to five times a week. One time I was so medicated that I wet the bed.

Many of my close friends worried about me. When I was thoroughly medicated, I tended to call my friends. I would ramble on, not making sense, and then not remember it the next day. I am grateful for those friends for putting up with me and my drugged-up rants. Sometimes I was so out of it that someone I was talking to actually came to my apartment to take me to the hospital ER. I have had charcoal (used to treat drug overdoses) on more than one occasion! My drugs definitely made my life crazy.

Step one is to admit to God that I am an addict and my drug use has made my life unmanageable. Easy! Anyone looking at my life could see my life had become unmanageable. Between the mental illness of bipolar disorder, the cutting, and the excessive overmedicating, my life was not fit to live. M was a good sponsor as she forced me to be honest about my drug use and how I had hurt myself and others.

Step four calls us to make restitution. It wasn't easy to tell past and present relationships that I was an addict and that I was wrong. The process was cleansing, but I did not have any earth-shattering experiences. The biggest restitution I had to make was with my mom. I tried to tell my mom of my experiences, NA, and my addictions. I told her that I wanted to make things right. I said that I would do my best to respect her. Mom was not impressed. She did not say much of anything—a simple "okay" was all I got.

NA turned out to be a great program for me. I learned to live with my emotions and stopped cutting and stopped abusing prescription medications. I have not cut in fourteen years as I write this. Part of me thinks that it feels like yesterday and time flew by. It doesn't seem like it has been fourteen years since I cut. And part of me thinks that it was a long process and am glad to have overcome.

When I was in my master's program, I had decided to do my thesis on the addiction of self-harming behavior. I thoroughly researched the topic and found that the evidence supported my hypothesis. I very much enjoyed writing that final paper. The dean of the Education Department told me that it was the best paper she had read in a very long time. She said that she had never thought of cutting (self-harm) as an addiction, and that I did a good job with my evidence.

The reason self-harming behavior is an addiction is because it fits the model of drug addiction. One, you have to take more and more in order to get the same high; and two, it Causes bodily distress to stop (withdrawal). Cutting usually starts off with small, superficial cuts and, as time goes on, it gets deeper and more often.

The circle of the self-harming behavior cycle goes like this: (1) The desire to self-harm getting increasingly strong; (2) thoughts of self-harm and plans of how to self-harm; (3) the self-harm takes place; (4) endorphins are released, and a calmness comes over the person; and (5) guilt sets in and the person feels bad which ultimately leads to the next cycle of self-harm. Sometimes the cycle takes hours, and other times it only takes minutes.

If you have never experienced the emotional pain that leads to self-harm and have never self-harmed, you will not understand the relief self-harm brings to a hurting soul. Not only does the physical pain distract you from emotional pain, but the physical pain releases the equivalent of eight milligrams of morphine into the brain which can bring a sense of euphoria. It isn't just "I cut myself so I feel better," but "I cut myself, and now I feel darn right good!" It is those "feel good" endorphins that make the cycle of self-harm very addictive.

I lived the NA program for about three years and decided I was well enough to stop going to meetings. They will tell you that you are an addict for life and you should attend meetings for the rest of your life. It's been fourteen years since I lived in my addictions, and I stopped going to meetings because I wanted to live a life not focused on my addictions, but a life full of service and joy. I still struggled with my mental illness for many years, but I had the building blocks and coping skills I needed to be able to live a more normal life. This is the first day of my future.

Light Enters the Darkness

When I first started going to the NA program, I found it very difficult to not cut and to not abuse drugs. I went through my apartment and threw away my box cutters and other razor blades I had around. I also disposed of all the extra medications that I was no longer prescribed. With temptation removed, I was able to focus on the program and my emotional baggage. I found M, my sponsor, to be helpful and caring but tough. She walked me through the twelve steps and encouraged me along the way. The NA program was the jumpstart to my recovery that I needed.

During the same time, I started a new therapy group that was based on Marsha Linehan, known as dialectical behavior therapy (DBT). DBT is used to treat self-harming behaviors. It was a year commitment with a group session and an individual session every week. In DBT, I learned a whole new set of coping skills. The most helpful skill I learned was mindfulness. The word is thrown around quite a bit today, but back then it was fairly new.

Mindfulness helps you to focus on the moment and to live in the present. The other skill I learned that helped a lot was distraction. If I was feeling strong urges to cut, I would do something—anything—to distract myself from what I was feeling. Self-soothing was also one of my go to skills. I would take a hot bath and put essential oils in the water. I especially liked lavender. It was not overnight, but by time the year was over, I felt I had a handle on my cutting.

When I started to feel some light in my life, I decided to go back to school. I still was fairly symptomatic, but it was manageable. I worked overnights in group homes and went to school three days a week from 6:00 p.m. to 9:00 p.m. What was nice about my job, working while the clients slept, was that I could study and do homework while working. I managed to stay out of the hospital for the two years I was in school. In 2008, I finally earned my M.Ed. (master's in education for guidance counseling).

I continued working in group homes through a temporary agency. I never did work in the school setting as the year I graduated was the year that they decided not to hire guidance counselors anymore—just spread out the ones they already had.

And in 2008, in December, Mike and I started dating. Mike was smart and could hold an intelligent conversation. He was caring and seemed to understand me. By May of 2009, we were a solid couple. I did have to tell Mike that I was mentally ill. Mike looked at me and said, "But you are not retarded!" I explained to him my history and my current situation as bipolar. I think that he must have also done some of his own research because he understood me very well as time went on. And despite some very bad ups and downs, he stuck by me!

We got married on May 21, 2010. Shortly after our marriage, I kind of had a small crash and told him that I wanted to go to the hospital. Mike looked at me and asked, "What does going to the hospital do for you?" I gave him my list:

1. I don't have to worry about my medications, as they are given to me at given time frames.
2. I don't have to go to work.
3. I don't have to cook dinner.
4. I don't have to worry about cleaning the house.
5. I can sleep as much as I want.

And so, the "hospital at home" was created. Mike took all my medications and locked them up. He would give me my daily medications when I was supposed to get them. He took my phone away from me and told me I was to stay in the house or backyard. I was no longer responsible for the care of the house or dinner. I was to call in sick to work.

After a couple of days, I was ready to go back to regular life. So I was "discharged." I utilized this "hospital at home" program a few times in our first year together. But through that program, I realized

I did not have to run to the hospital for every wild emotion! I could work through my emotions at home and with Mike's help. I have not been in the hospital since 2009 and have never had to go back to using the "hospital at home."

My life now is so opposite from all the darkness and confusion I once lived in. I started going to Springs Chapel with my aunt Helga in 2011. Right off the bat I started serving where I was needed. My first week in chapel someone announced that they needed someone to print the bulletin. So I took on that task. The bulletin was emailed to me every week, and I took it down to the UPS store to print it. Five or six years later, I took on actually typing up the bulletin and prayer sheets. I still print them with a fellow member's help, but in my home, not at the UPS store any longer. And this past year, I took on doing the prayer chain. I very much enjoy serving the Chapel!

In general, I try to be a servant. So many helped me through my bad years, and now, I want to help others. Mostly it comes in the form of driving seniors in my community to doctor appointments, grocery shopping, or other tasks. I also make myself available to help those in my community do anything they may need done. Serving others helps me stay humble and keeps me out of my head.

People ask me, "What made you get better?" One of the biggest things that helped me was to have an "attitude of gratitude," which is something I learned in NA. Also, studying my Bible and praying, and having good Christian friends have been a big source of light in my life. And finally, serving others has helped me to understand what is normal. In serving others, they share with me their lives which I can then apply to mine.

I have come to understand that everyone has issues, but we don't have to let those issues overwhelm us and take over our minds. Yes, I still am medicated, but I am stable and no longer change medications every time I go see the doctor. The medication addresses the chemical imbalance, friends help me address the social aspect of mental illness, and God helps me address the spiritual realm of it all.

MY LAST BIG FALL

Problems

Shortly after I graduated with my master's degree, I got engaged to Mike. I then had one of the worst depressive episodes that I had ever had. I had to switch clinics since I had moved, so I ended up with a new doctor. And when I say "new," I mean new! She introduced herself as NP, and that she recently graduated, and that this was her first job as a physician's assistant.

My case manager from the old clinic met with me and my new case manager and gave a basic history. The most important part of my history was my medication, namely the Haldol D injection that I had been allowed to ask for when I needed it as I had good insight to my illness.

A month later, I came into the clinic and asked for a Haldol D injection. I was feeling off. I was not sleeping, I was depressed, and I wasn't thinking clearly. NP saw me on an emergency basis, but she would not allow me the Haldol D injection. She said that it would interfere with my Cymbalta (antidepressant). I had been on Cymbalta for six months and had a couple of Haldol D injections and never had an issue. NP would not budge. I told her about my history of anti-depressants and Haldol D, but to no avail. She refused to listen to me.

I asked her to read my chart as it was well documented that this medicine helped me significantly. She said that she was not going to read my chart and that I needed to trust that she knew what was best. I was in tears because I knew that there was not another medication that had the dramatic effect that the Haldol D had. Any time I had been hospitalized and was given Haldol D, I improved quickly. I felt the stability that I had worked so hard for slipping through my fingers.

I was working on my second master's degree in 2009 and only had about three weeks of my classes for that semester left. Because of my instability and my inability to get the medication that would clear my mind, I was asked to withdraw from school. Well, actually I was told that the dean of the counseling department was going to withdraw me as I needed to take care of myself. A whole semester of work was lost!

I scheduled another appointment with NP, as I was slipping rather quickly into a world of darkness, psychosis, and confusion. My mom came with me to this appointment so she could advocate for me. NP again said that she would not read my history. "Our bodies change over time, so I am starting over with her medications." My mom tried to convince NP to just read my chart, and NP said that she wasn't going to waste her time reading my chart.

My mom was angry at NP! She started yelling and cussing at her. I kept telling my mom to stop yelling at NP. I finally could see we were not getting anywhere, so I led my mom out as she was still yelling at NP. I was worried that if she kept on, they would call the police and either have her arrested or committed!

The next day, I went back to the clinic to ask for help. I was crying and not able to make much sense. I asked my case manager for help to get me into the hospital. My case manager said that she was not going to help me do something that I could do myself. I begged for help and explained that I couldn't do what it took to get into the hospital. Eventually, I just went out to the parking lot and sat on the curb. Eventually, Mike came to pick me up as I didn't think I could drive.

I explained to Mike what was happening with my medications. I told him that I was disassociating (mind was not connected to my body) and that I could not feel my body. Mike asked if he could help. I told him that I would sign a release of information so that he could talk to the clinic. In the meantime, I filed a grievance.

I asked for a different doctor, but they denied the request. I called the clinic and spoke with the clinic manager. I explained what was going on and asked him, "What, is the doctor God in your clinic? If the doctor orders something, that's it? It's written in stone?"

The manager said, "Yes, basically. The doctor is in charge of an individual's treatment."

I called to schedule another emergency appointment. It was scheduled for two weeks out. I explained that I was in crisis and I needed help, now! They said I could see the nurse tomorrow. I took that appointment. But then, I received a phone call that day, about thirty minutes before my appointment, telling me that my appointment had been cancelled. No reason was given. I tried to schedule another one. They said that it had to go through the doctor. I was going in circles.

I became very suicidal. I had a plan. I was going to take a bottle of Vicodin (pain medication) and a bottle of Atenolol (blood pressure medication) and go sit in the hot tub in our community. I figured I would pass out and then drown. I talked to Mike about my thoughts. He decided enough was enough, and he took me to the hospital himself.

I was admitted to the hospital. It was night time, so all I did was be evaluated and admitted. I was shown to my room, and I laid down and just cried myself to sleep. How could I have come so far down?

The next day, I met my doctor. She was a nice lady but completely non-understanding of my situation. I told her that I just needed some Haldol D, and I would be better. She said that she had talked to my outpatient provider, and they were not on board with giving me Haldol D or oral Haldol. She put me on Risperdal.

I told Mike about my new medication change. He tried to advocate for me at the family meeting, but to no avail. They were going to keep me on Risperdal and set me up with outpatient hospitalization at St. Luke. They would pick me up five days a week for program and drop me off at home every evening. Lunch would be provided. There was no use of staying inpatient, so after about a week, I was discharged to outpatient intensive hospitalization.

At St. Luke, I met up with Dr. B, the doctor that diagnosed me after I had ECT. He understood that I had bipolar disorder (with mild psychotic features), and he agreed that I needed to be on Haldol. He said he would contact the clinic provider and try to get me put back on Haldol.

My clinic provider was standing strong about not using Haldol. She insisted that I was just being stubborn and acting out to get what I want. Who on earth wants Haldol? It is not a drug you get high on. It is not a drug people ask for! It is a drug with some very bad side effects. I just knew it worked for me. But this NP was not going to give it to me for any reason!

I participated in the outpatient hospital groups, but I could not concentrate, and I was severely suicidal. Mike had filed several grievances on my behalf, and I was promised a new doctor. That never materialized. Mike tried talking to the people who oversaw the grievance department. Again, to no avail. I could not fight anymore. I was done.

I sat in the last group of the day writing out my plan to kill my case manager and then myself. I figured I had no choice but to kill myself, and if I was going to die, I was taking someone with me. I wrote my plan. I was going to ask my case manager to go for a walk. As we walked, I was going to pull out my box cutter, grab her arm, and slice her neck. I would then, in one fluid motion, slice my own neck. *Bam.* Done. Maybe then they would understand what they had done to me.

I was supposed to get on the van to come home. Not sure I was ready to pull off my plan, I decided that I was not going to go home. In fact, I was not going to ever be seen again. I kept walking. I had every right to not get on the van. I would walk into the night and become a homeless person. I was just so tired of fighting.

Meanwhile, St. Luke's staff called Mike, my emergency contact. They told him I did not get on the van, and I had walked away. They did not know where I was going. We were pretty close to the VA hospital, so I ended up walking to the VA hospital and sitting down for a break. This was not a safe area of town; but I did not care. I then walked across the street to Subway to get something to eat.

47

I pondered my situation. I could keep going and just be a nameless, homeless person, or I could call Mike. God must have been watching out for me. Without knowing where I was, Mike prayed that God would guide him to me. This was before the days of GPS tracking. Then the most amazing thing happened next. Mike walked through the door to Subway and saw me sitting there. He said, "What the hell do you think you are doing?"

Crying, I stated, "I don't know. I just can't do this anymore." I was so grateful to see Mike but also scared that I would be forced to keep fighting.

Mike opened my notebook and saw the letter I had written about killing the case manager and then myself. He said, "I am taking you back to the hospital." We drove mostly in silence with me in tears. When we arrived at the psychiatric hospital, Mike gave the intake lady the letter I had written. She then faxed that letter to my clinic. Since I was voluntarily asking for help, they could not court order me as they had done in the past. But since I was homicidal and suicidal, I was admitted.

I was expecting to get the same doctor as I had last time, but instead I got a different doctor. I thought, "Maybe there is hope." I told the doctor my desire to be given Haldol (oral) as it has always worked in the past. I was smart—I had ordered my records from the outpatient clinic. Mike brought them to the hospital to give to my doctor. She said she would go over the records and go from there. Again I thought, "Maybe there is hope."

Meanwhile, I was restricted to the unit with a one-to-one sitter. I knew the drill as this was normal for me. When I was told I had to go to group, I started to throw a tantrum. It was stupid. I managed to de-escalate myself before I was taken down and put in restraints.

After being in the hospital for a week, my old case manager came through the door. He was a psychiatric technician and was working on my ward that day. I told him the whole crazy story of trying to get some Haldol. He said that he would be happy to talk to the doctor and tell her that he saw first-hand that Haldol works for me. Once again I thought, "Maybe there is hope."

And yes, the doctor did decide to try the oral Haldol. It was an amazing change. Overnight, my mind cleared up and the intense darkness went away. They had a family meeting to decide my discharge date. The doctor was pleased that I had done so well on the Haldol and was ready to discharge me. Problem was, I had to see the psychiatrist at my clinic within seventy-two hours. Did they forget I had threatened to kill the case manager there? I could not go back to that clinic!

Mike called the grievance line to try to get my case transferred to another clinic. They said, "We are sorry, but a transfer takes up to ninety days." Mike was furious. They wanted me to go back to the clinic that caused all the problems in the first place. Mike asked them, "What if she were new to the system, and she was being discharged?"

They said, "Well, she would be assigned a clinic and seen within seventy-two hours."

Mike said, "Then pretend she is a new patient." They seemed to finally get it. They walked my files over to the new clinic that day! And I was discharged the evening before Thanksgiving when every detail was worked out. That was the first day of my future.

That was eleven years ago. They have increased my Haldol every so often, but my basic regimen has stayed the same since that time. When I get a new case manager, I am sure to tell him/her the basics of my story to help them understand how bad things can get without Haldol. I also talk to my doctor when he/she changes to make sure that they don't change my medication. I am happy to say I have not been hospitalized since then, and I have only had mild mood changes that I tell my doctor about right away.

HELPING OTHERS

How to Help Those Experiencing Mental Health Issues

In 2000, I graduated with my BA in psychology, and in 2008, I graduated with my M. Ed. in guidance counseling. I worked in the mental health field for over ten years. And to top it off, I was one of the worst mental health patients at one time. So I feel I am qualified to explain to others how to help people who are experiencing mental health issues.

First and foremost, you want to be sure the person is physically safe. Whether they self-harm or are suicidal, you want to assess the level of danger. If the person says they want to hurt themselves, do they have the means and the motive? For example, does the person have a knife, razor blades, or lots of pills in their possession? If this is a yes, and they are expressing a strong motivation for using them, find a way to get those items out of their possession.

S often kept my extra medications locked in a tool box and in his closet. He gave me one day to two days at a time. You can never create the perfectly safe environment, but you can take the obvious items with which the person can harm themselves. Sometimes the very act of getting rid of dangerous items is therapeutic. It empowers the person to feel like they are taking charge of their safety.

It may seem intrusive to ask a person, "Do you want to kill yourself?" But upfront, honesty actually shows that you care. Trust me, a severely depressed person, whether they admit it or not, has had those thoughts on more than one occasion. Go with your gut. If you sense the person is in danger, *ask them*! You may save a life.

Not all mental illness is about safety. This is an extreme that hopefully you won't have to deal with. The most important thing that a person with mental health issues needs is a good friend. Someone they can confide in and know that isn't going anywhere. Listen! And honestly, the most important thing you can do for someone with mental illness is share things you are grateful for so you can give them ideas of things they can be grateful for.

Gratitude lifts the spirit. Encourage the person to pray and read their bible. I know that, in my story, I have stated that being told to pray and read my scriptures did not help; and, by themselves, they don't. What helps is to be a true friend and offer to share scriptures with them and/or to pray with them. On many occasions, when the person offering scripture help or prayer was a friend first and spiritual guider second, it made a difference—at least, in the moment.

I can't stress enough how important friendship is as opposed to empty spiritual advice. The book of Psalms always touched my heart when I was struggling. The author of Psalms suffered greatly and always came out the other side a better person.

Praying with someone who is struggling can be so helpful.

> The prayer of a righteous person is powerful
> and effective. (James 5:16 NIV)

So many times when I didn't know what to do and the friend that I was pouring my heart out to didn't know what to do, going before the King of heaven and leaving the mess at his feet is the best thing I could do.

Don't just tell the person to pray about it. Ask the person if you can pray for them right then and there. Be sensitive. Asking someone to pray can be met with resistance, especially if they feel at odds with God. If they are not ready to pray or allow you to pray with them, simply say a prayer in your heart for that person and drop it.

Once, I had a client who was just losing all composure. She was screaming and crying. I could not pray with her as it was a state-run program. My heart just broke for her, but I left her alone and prayed on my own for her. Eventually, she calmed down and went to sleep. I believe God answered my prayer and does answer prayers in time.

Mental illness is difficult to grasp, especially the suffering that goes along with it. But ultimately, we must remember: God is sovereign. We are each created for a purpose, and we each will face trials. And until the last trial is faced and our purpose is lived, we will continue to go forward. Today is the first day of our future.

ABOUT THE AUTHOR

Dionna Reeb grew up in a single-parent Christian home. Mental health issues began to present in her life at about age ten. It was not until her young twenties that the depression and self-harm really began to take over her life.

Even with multiple hospitalizations, she managed to get her BA in psychology in 2000 and her M.Ed in guidance counseling from Ottawa University in 2008. Dionna's marriage to Michael Reeb in 2010 made a huge difference in her stability. Now she is helping neighbors in her community with transportation to doctor appointments, shopping, and incidentals.

CPSIA information can be obtained
at www.ICGtesting.com
Printed in the USA
JSHW041211220421
13798JS00002B/77

9 781636 309224